IS IT GERMANY OR DEUTSCHLAND?

GEOGRAPHY 4TH GRADE CHILDREN'S EUROPE BOOKS

In this book, we're going to talk about exploring the country of **GERMANY**. So, let's get right to it!

WHERE IS GERMANY?

Germany is located in the center of Europe. It has coastline along the North Sea to the northwest and the Baltic Sea to the northeast. It also shares a border with Denmark at its northern tip. Traveling counterclockwise from west to east, the other countries that have borders that touch Germany's are the Netherlands, Belgium, Luxembourg, France, Switzerland, Austria, the Czech Republic, and Poland.

Germany has nine countries that share its borders. It shares more borders than any other country in Europe.

WHAT ARE THE GEOGRAPHIC AND NATURAL FEATURES OF GERMANY?

Germany has great natural beauty and its terrain varies in different regions. In the northern part of the country, the terrain becomes a wide flat plain that extends out to the North Sea.

Germany's major rivers—the Danube River, the Elbe River, and the Rhine River—cut through the west, east, and south of the country. The central region and the southern region of the country have mountainous terrain with dense forests.

DANUBE RIVER

LAKE TITISEE, BLACK FOREST

Germany's most famous forest is located close to the Swiss border. It's the Black Forest, which is filled with fir trees as well as pine trees and is the source of the Danube, one of the longest rivers in Europe.

WILD BOAR

The forests and mountains of the south provide habitats for wildcats and boars and the northern coast is home to sea creatures and migrating birds.

WHAT IS THE CULTURE LIKE IN GERMANY?

The word "Germany" came from the word "Germania" in Latin. The Gauls used this word to describe the country first. Later, Julius Caesar and his Roman Empire used the word "Germany" to describe the country. However, the German people use the word "Deutschland" for their homeland instead of Germany.

JULIUS CAESAR

JOHANN SEBASTIAN BACH

Today, Germany has a mixture of populations since 10% of the people who live there are from another country. Many Turkish people came to Germany in the 1950s seeking work. About 60% of the population is Christian.

The German people have become famous for all different art forms and Deutschland has always been known for both its great poets and its great thinkers. Germany is also known for its many famous musicians and classical composers such as Johann Sebastian Bach, Johannes Brahms, and Ludwig Van Beethoven.

WHAT IS THE HISTORY OF GERMANY?

Human beings have been living in the northern part of Europe since about 10,000 years ago. The first population that spoke a language that is similar in structure and vocabulary as the German language that is spoken today were living there around 5,000 years ago. However, it took many thousands of years before the country would be established with its modern borders.

Th. Kalbfuss
J.A.ZOEPPRITZ.
L.&M.Fuld.

In ancient times, Germany was a group of different states that were not unified. These varying states were ruled by a series of dukes and kings. However, the country's history changed when a politician by the name of Otto von Bismarck came on the scene. He united the country into one Deutschland in 1871 by using both diplomacy and force.

OTTO VON BISMARCK

GERMAN ARMY

Around 1900, Germany was in competition with other countries of Europe to establish colonies on the continents of Asia as well as Africa. The conflicts among the nations of Europe led to World War I beginning in 1914. The countries of Britain, the United States, and France battled against Germany in the First World War and Germany lost.

The German people were fiercely proud of their nation. When Adolf Hitler and his Nazi Regime seized power in the year 1933, he told the people that they would build Germany up to its former glory. Hitler hated the Jewish people because he felt they had caused Germany to lose World War I. He wanted the German people to develop a pure Aryan race and to expand the space they had for ensuring this race would succeed.

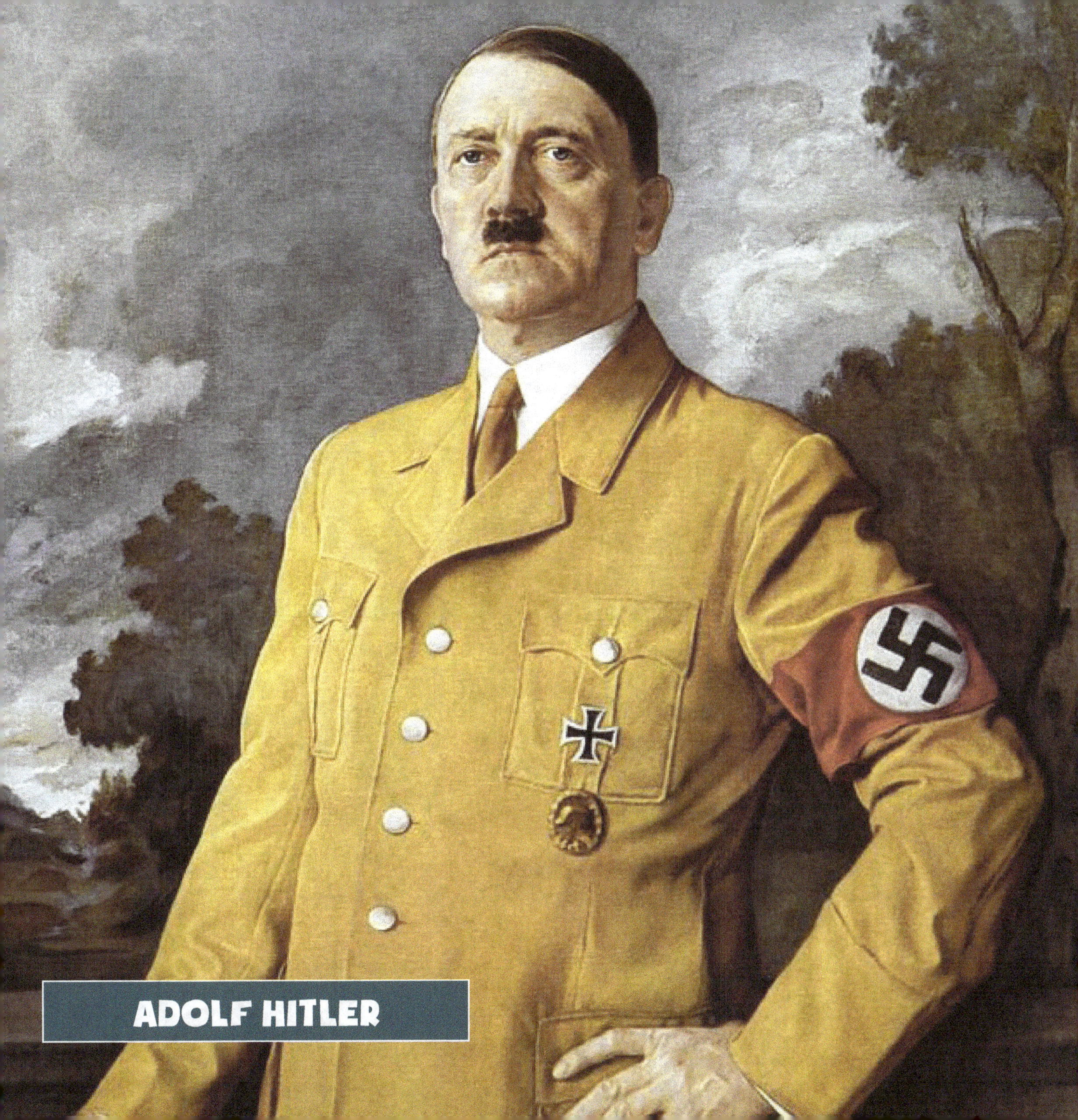
ADOLF HITLER

Hitler invaded its next-door neighbor Poland in 1939, which was the beginning of World War II. During the war, Hitler established concentration camps where millions of Jewish people were killed. Germany was defeated in 1945 and the German people have had to live with the truth of his "crimes against humanity" ever since that time.

After the Second World War, the Allied Powers divided Germany into two countries, West and East. During the Cold War, the country was at the core of the tense relationship between the Soviet Union, which had possession of the East, and the United States and its allies, which had possession of the West.

Then, toward the end of the 1980s, the Eastern European nations began to revolt against the communist leadership of the Soviets. The wall between East Germany and West Germany came down in 1989 and the Soviet Union collapsed in 1991 signaling the end of the Cold War.

WHAT PLACES ARE GOOD FOR EXPLORING IN GERMANY?

There are so many exciting places to visit in Germany. Here are just a few of the many places you may enjoy visiting.

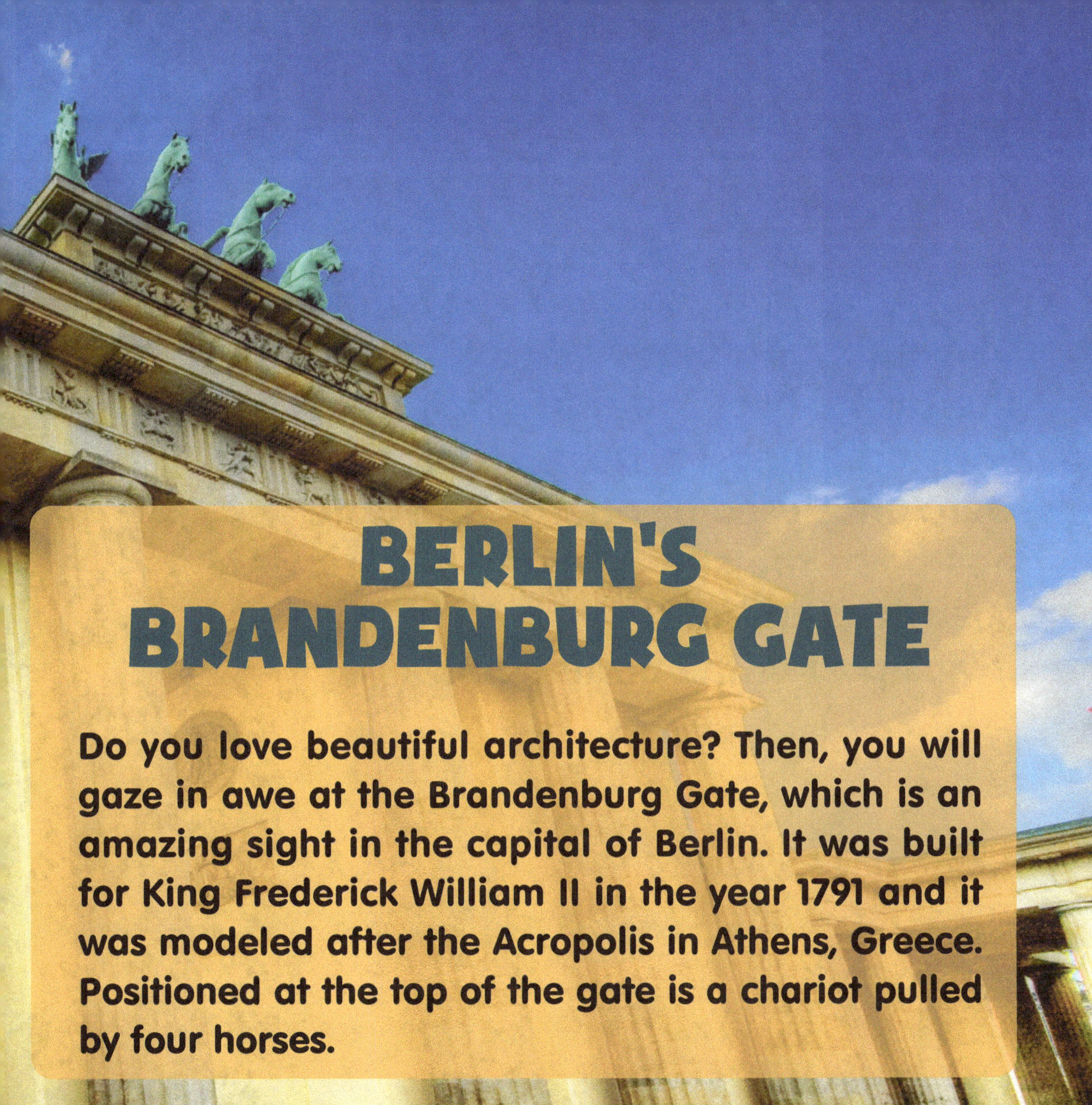

BERLIN'S BRANDENBURG GATE

Do you love beautiful architecture? Then, you will gaze in awe at the Brandenburg Gate, which is an amazing sight in the capital of Berlin. It was built for King Frederick William II in the year 1791 and it was modeled after the Acropolis in Athens, Greece. Positioned at the top of the gate is a chariot pulled by four horses.

This amazing statue is supported above six 26-meter-high columns in the Doric style. There are buildings with columns on both sides that were once used by guards. The gate has been the site of many historic speeches and during the Cold War it was part of the Berlin Wall.

01 519
SCHWARZWALDBAHN

THE BLACK FOREST

Would you like to see a gigantic cuckoo clock? Then, you'll love visiting the Black Forest. You can travel by car through the scenic valleys and dense, dark forests. In the central part of the forest you can take the Black Forest Railway, called the Schwarzwaldbahn in German, which travels for 150 kilometers.

TRIBERG

Another beautiful place to see is Triberg, known for its spectacular waterfalls. Triberg also has the Black Forest Museum or Schwarzwald Museum with eighteen different rooms that display the traditions and culture of the region. When you travel to the tiny town of Schonach, you can see its famous cuckoo clock, which is the largest such clock in the world. Another interesting place to visit is near Gutach. It is the Open Air Museum. The buildings located there are farmhouses that date back to the 1600s.

THE FAIRYTALE CASTLE OF NEUSCHWANSTEIN

Would you like to see a real-life fairytale castle? Then, you'll want to visit the Neuschwanstein Castle near the town of Füssen in the German section of the Alps. This incredible castle was used as a model for the castles that Walt Disney had built in his theme parks. It was built between 1869 and 1886 for a Bavarian king--King Ludwig II.

The interior is filled with amazing rooms such as the Throne Room and the Singer's Hall. The view from the castle of the surrounding mountains and forests is spectacular.

THRONE ROOM
THRONE ROOM

MINIATUR WUNDERLAND

THE MINIATUR WUNDERLAND

Would you like to see an amazing model railway? Then, you will want to travel to historic Hamburg to see the Miniatur Wunderland. It is an amazing scale model railroad, the largest of its kind in the world. It has more than 12,000 meters of track, over 890 trains, over 200,000 human figures, and more than 300,000 lights!

   In addition to having a section showing Hamburg, it also has a section that shows the United States as well as Scandinavia. Trains are not the only mode of transportation in this scale model. It has miniature airports with planes that actually take off on its model runways! It has beautiful scenes such as quaint rural settings and miniature harbors.

AIRPORT, MINIATUR WUNDERLAND HAMBURG

HARBOR AT HAMBURG

In addition to this amazing miniature world within the city, Hamburg has beautiful places to walk such as the harborside promenade. You can take a boat trip to see the actual harbor once you've seen the miniature ones.

INSEL MAINAU

Do you love flowers? Then, you will want to travel to the scenic Insel Mainau, which is a beautiful island of flowers on Lake Constance in the southern part of Germany. Many visitors come here every year to explore the over 100 acres of plants from around the world including lush tropical and semitropical plants.

INSEL MAINAU

You can get to the island by taking a boat or you can walk over a bridge built for pedestrians from the mainland. The island has 30,000 rose bushes with 1,200 varieties of roses. There is a greenhouse that has thousands of butterflies.

SUMMARY

From the majestic Bavarian Alps to the Black Forest to the coastlines of the North and Baltic Seas, Germany is a country of incredible natural beauty. Although its history has been scarred by both World Wars as well as the Cold War, its people are once again united both east and west and are finally free of both Nazi and Soviet rule. There are many beautiful places to visit in this country that has been central to Europe's history, culture, art, and music.

BAVARIAN ALPS

Awesome! Now that you've gone exploring in Germany, you may want to visit the country of Canada in the Baby Professor book **Does It Always Snow in Canada? Geography 4th Grade.**

Visit

BABY PROFESSOR
EDUCATION KIDS

www.BabyProfessorBooks.com
to download Free Baby Professor eBooks
and view our catalog of new and exciting
Children's Books